FACING CANCER WITH MARY

Reflections, prayers *and* spiritual practices

CATHERINE STEWART, OP

TWENTY-THIRD PUBLICATIONS
twentythirdpublications.com

TWENTY-THIRD PUBLICATIONS
One Montauk Avenue, Suite 200
New London, CT 06320
(860) 437-3012 or (800) 321-0411
www.twentythirdpublications.com

Cover photo: ©Shutterstock.com / Thoom

ISBN: 978-1-62785-349-1
Library of Congress Control Number: 2017961011
Printed in the U.S.A.

 A division of Bayard, Inc.

CONTENTS

ACKNOWLEDGMENTS

*If the only prayer you said in your whole life
was "thank you," that would suffice.*

MEISTER ECKHART

I am deeply grateful to Dr. Paul E. Pacheco, who accepted me as a transfer patient and performed emergency surgery that saved my life. His kindness, compassion, and willingness to listen are gifts I shall always treasure. He will always be in my "Gratitude Litany" and to this day, I stay in touch with him. Dr. Brad Paris assisted Dr. Pacheco; I am also grateful for his expertise.

Dr. Amit Gupta and Brittney Veenstra, APN, and their staff walked with me throughout my entire chemotherapy journey. They always had time to answer my questions, to encourage me when I experienced "down days," and to rejoice with me when all was going well. They too are always in my prayers of gratitude. I moved to Fond du Lac, Wisconsin, and Dr. Jones took over my "maintenance care." I am grateful for his willingness to step into the middle of my story. He and his staff are filled with compassion and positive outlooks as I continue the journey as a survivor.

Until I walked this journey, I never knew the warm compassion and caring that I found in the many doctors, nurses, residents, interns, aides, medical testing personnel, and receptionists. I am grateful for their overwhelming kindness, their pats on the shoulder, and their words of comfort. All of them are tucked in my prayers of thanksgiving.

How do I begin to thank my family and friends? All of them seemed to anticipate my many needs: hugs, encouraging words, quiet visits, flowers; together we deepened each other's faith as we walked through the questions into the answers.

The Dominican Sisters of Springfield, Illinois, supported me in so many ways. Some drove me to numerous doctor appointments and chemotherapy treatments. So many of them stopped for daily visits as I recuperated in our full-care facility. Many of them prayed with and for me during the long journey of recovery. Others slowly walked the long halls with me as I worked to regain my strength. I am so grateful for their presence in my life.

A special thanks to Father Mark Osterhaus, Sister Paul Bernadette Bounc, and Father Ronald Margherio who read the "rough manuscript" and suggested I send it to Twenty-Third Publications for possible publication. Once it was accepted, these three helped me get over "my cold feet" as I realized the magnitude of what I had begun.

Naturally, all of the people at Twenty-Third Publications are in my litany of gratitude. Trish Vanni and Dan Connors once again gave me gentle suggestions as we prepared the manuscript for publication.

INTRODUCTION

I never imagined that one day I would be a cancer survivor. My life journey was filled with relationships—family, friends, acquaintances, educational degrees, a deep love for God and the people of God, a passion for teaching, and a love for all life holds.

I walked two miles every day, I ate well and lived a fairly balanced life. I made sure I had routine tests and my annual physical. My doctor once commented that if his income depended on me, he would be penniless. An occasional cold was my only illness.

Mom and I were vacationing in Kentucky for a week. We rented a cabin on the lake and enjoyed card games, reading novels, and walking around the lake. It was the perfect getaway. Toward the middle of the week, I began to feel ill. I thought it was a routine urinary tract infection. Once we returned to Illinois, I went to a walk-in clinic, and after a few tests the doctor diagnosed it as a urinary tract infection, and I was given an antibiotic. A couple of days passed, and I wasn't feeling any better. After our family picnic, I called my brother and asked him and his wife to take me to the emergency room; I expected to see a doctor, receive a stronger antibiotic, and be sent home. After several hours, I was admitted to the hospital for further testing.

I was in a small hospital for a few days and then transferred to a much larger hospital for more testing. It was during one of these tests that I became extremely ill as the surgeon was explaining the results of the test; he realized I immediately needed surgery. I was rushed to the operating room.

As a cancer patient and survivor, I often choose to walk in the footsteps of Mary through the framework of the mysteries of the Rosary. The mysteries help us focus on Mary's life. Mary was a strong and courageous woman—she lived in darkness at times when she was unsure of where her journey was taking her. She grew in her relationships—small steps at a time. She lived in the present and tried to respond to the moment at hand, trusting that saying "yes" in small everyday ways would deepen her faith and assuage the doubts that lurked within.

The reflections in this book are centered on my cancer journey. At times, your journey will mirror mine, and at other times your experiences will be very different. Through connecting to my story and my reflections on Mary's journey, I hope the "Spirit" touches your heart and assists you in embracing your journey with poignant moments of laughter, tears, and hope.

THE
JOYFUL
MYSTERIES

THE **ANNUNCIATION**

Saying the first yes of many yeses to follow

Mary's life took an unexpected turn as she was visited by the Angel Gabriel. I often wonder if she felt overwhelmed, dazed, puzzled, and confused after Gabriel left. Did she wonder how her "yes" would impact not just her present life but her future as well? Like Mary, my life was about to take an unexpected turn as the surgeon, "Dr. P," said, "I'm going to get an operating room and we're going to do surgery NOW!" As he left, I was scared and confused; I didn't really understand what was happening.

I was rushed off to emergency surgery at 4:30 pm on

August 6, 2014, the Feast of the Transfiguration. Little did I know how this feast would impact my future. My family (my mom, brothers, sister-in-law, and sister) and religious community were called and arrived as quickly as possible, but I was already in surgery. The waiting began for them. I was in surgery until 10:30 pm. After surgery Dr. P informed my family and religious community there was a cancerous tumor; he removed it and most of the colon and created an ileostomy. Some lymph nodes were involved. I had stage III colon cancer, and my condition was guarded; if emergency surgery had not occurred, I would have died. My brother and sister-in-law stayed until I came out of recovery. The ICU nurse untangled numerous tubes and explained to them what each one did for me. They left knowing I was in good hands.

The next morning, I heard a voice say, "Catherine, it's time to wake up." As soon as I awoke, I felt hot. I couldn't talk, but the nurse said I would be able to in a few minutes, after they took me off the ventilator. Later, Dr. P came in to check on me and gave me the same information he had given my family the night before. I was surprised—I knew I wasn't feeling well, but I didn't think I was that ill. I don't think at this point I really understood how ill I was. I only knew I was in a lot of pain.

I was heavily sedated during the first few days, and as I drifted in and out of sleep, I wondered, Where does courage come from? Do I have enough of it? What in my past prepared me for this journey? I know all experiences are connected. Each experience prepares us for the next step. How is my faith going to help me through this? What if my faith doesn't help? What do I do with the fact that I almost died? What does it mean to have cancer? How does an ileostomy change my life? My life journey was about to take a whole new route. I wasn't sure how to be ill; I had always been healthy, full of energy, and very independent. Now, I had tubes, machines, nurses, doctors, residents, interns, and lots of other hospital personnel.

As the days passed, the pain lessened, and I became more aware of my situation. I wasn't asking a lot of questions; I was content to just "be." Dr. P stopped by one morning and said, "Oh, so this is what you look like when you are feeling better—there's a twinkle in your eye."

I was in ICU for nine days. At one point, Dr. P checked in on me, and I asked him, "Could I please have some ice chips?" He nodded and said yes. I replied, "Thanks—it's like Christmas in August." Dr. P laughed and said "Wow, you must be a very simple woman if that's all it takes to make you happy." I quickly replied, "Yes, I'm content with just little things."

A few days later, Dr. P said, "Catherine, your heart rate is a bit fast; are you anxious and would you like something for it?" I replied, "Yes, I'm anxious I don't know what the world is going to be like when I'm better, but no, I don't want any medicine for anxiety—I just have to reach deeper inside for the answer. I just need time to process what I know and try to figure out how I will cope. I think I can do this." Some people would gladly accept the medication, but I just didn't want any more drugs. I still was taking pain medication and that was enough!

Dr. P stopped in to check on me every day during my time in ICU, and every day I would ask "What gift do I get today?" He bestowed red popsicles, soft food, regular food, and his last gifts to me were a shower with getting my hair washed, and getting discharged from the hospital. I was blessed, because upon discharge, I was able to go to our skilled nursing care facility at our motherhouse. I was fortunate. Others who have this experience must look for short-term care covered by their insurance or arrange for home health care.

My days in the hospital gave me a deeper awareness of seeing the extraordinary in the ordinary. No longer did I take anything for granted. All was gift! I became aware of a community of compassionate healers. A group of residents stopped in to see me every morning around 7 am. I tried to be semi-awake so I could be somewhat hospitable and answer their questions. Everyone on my health care team helped me as I began to heal. I felt safe, secure, and optimistic. I quietly said "yes" as I began the journey of a cancer patient. I did not know where the journey would take me, but I did know I had the support of doctors, nurses, family, religious community, and friends. I also knew God walked with me.

Mary's journey began much in the same way. She was doing ordinary, routine chores when she suddenly experienced God's presence in a deeper way. We do not know if she said yes immediately to Gabriel's request or if she paused for a bit and then said yes. We do not know if it was a whispered yes that was barely audible or if it was a strong yes. We do not know if Mary was aware of all of the implications that were to grow from her initial yes. I suspect she didn't know. When we reflect on the many yeses we've uttered in our lifetimes, most of the time we had no idea how the first yes was going to evolve into other yeses.

So often we search for God; we look for felt experiences of him, and yet it is God who initiates the relationship—we are found by him. In looking back over our lives, we become aware of being found by God as we silently contemplate a sunrise or sunset; we are found by God when we experience overwhelming gratitude at the birth of a child; we are found by God when tears of sadness roll down our cheeks at the loss of a loved one; we are found by God when we see the tenderness of love. Our ordinary lives are filled with moments of being found by God, and it is in this awareness that our yes emerges.

Prayer

Good and Gracious God, thank you for the many people in our lives who modeled saying yes when you called them to begin a new journey. Help us to become aware of the many gifts in our lives that support our yes, no matter how tentative or how strong it is. When our "yes" is barely whispered, send someone to remind us of Mary's deep faith. Give us the grace to acknowledge our fear and uncertainty, and fill us with peace as we reach out to our health care team.

Journal experience

Reflect on the major yeses you have said up to this point. Create a time line with these yeses. As you think about them, is there a pattern? Do you say yes tentatively at first and then as the journey continues does your yes become surer and louder? Do you jump in with a resounding yes! that deepens as your journey continues?

THE **VISITATION**

Supporting each other in our vulnerability

I n the Annunciation, the angel Gabriel told Mary that her cousin Elizabeth was pregnant. Immediately after, Mary left to go and help her. When she met Elizabeth, both women were filled with gratitude for gifts God bestowed on each of them. Each woman reached deep within to find the courage needed to continually say yes to the next part of the journey.

As I walked in the footsteps of Mary, my visitation experience was a bit different. Friends and family visited me in ICU as often as they were allowed, even though I didn't remember the visits during the first few days. My mom was in assisted living and no longer drove, so my brother picked her up and brought her to visit. Mom said, "Catherine, if I had known you were this sick, I would have driven us home from Kentucky"; my mom is always a selfless giver.

During these visits, we often chatted about the ordinary things everyone was doing. We teased about the "nest of pillows" I had—two under the arm that had an IV in it, one tucked over my abdomen, so I could hold it if I had to cough, and two more tucked between me and the bed rail; I created a nest in which I felt safe and secure. I made a rule that most people who have abdominal surgery would make: "Don't make me laugh—it hurts!" Little by little, tubes and machines were removed. I was feeling better and was receiving less pain medication. I was able to get up and walk around a bit, but I was too weak to walk very far. I am an avid reader, so everyone made sure I was surrounded by reading material.

How excited I was the day I was discharged. I knew I still had a long road of recovery ahead, but I was ready to begin the journey. My belongings were packed, and flowers were given to patients who stayed behind. A wheelchair was readied. I smiled, waved goodbye to my medical team, and carefully placed myself in the wheelchair. One of the hospital volunteers took me down to the waiting car. The ride across the city was bumpy and painful. Up to this moment, I had had a pillow to put across my abdomen to give support. No one thought to bring a pillow along!

Upon arrival at our motherhouse, a nurse was waiting with a wheelchair and carefully took me to my room in our full-care nursing facility. She helped me get settled, and I took a nice long nap.

I had to adjust to a new routine, and I soon learned the names of the nurses and aides. All of them were very caring and looked out for my best interests. I learned that I intuitively knew when I was ready for the next step in my healing process. I was continually amazed at how weak I was. I was used to walking two miles in twenty-eight minutes; now, I could barely walk fifty feet. Every morning, afternoon, and evening, I was up and trying to walk a bit farther than the time before.

Friends and family continued to visit, as did the retired sisters. I also had visits from the home healthcare nurses who changed my wound dressings and began to teach me about my stoma. My stoma was short and stumpy and had a bit of a droop—it reminded me of Fred Flinstone, so I named it Fred. At first I was scared of Fred. I thought I might hurt him if I ate the wrong things or bumped him. My "yes" at this time was very tentative. Learning how to take care of Fred was a major ordeal. There wasn't anything that came naturally. I needed lots of help from our nursing staff as I learned how to empty Fred's house and how to burp Fred when necessary. I also had to learn how to give Fred a bath, powder and spray the skin around him, and apply a new "house." I remember my stoma nurse,

Mari, holding me as I cried and said "Dying would have been easier; I didn't sign up for this." Mari cried with me. After this meltdown, I took a deep breath and said "OK, let's do this."

However, after Mari left, I was still in meltdown mode. Most of the afternoon and evening found me "cloudy with a chance of tears." By the next morning, I had once again regained my balance and was ready to face the next challenge. Slowly I became adept at taking care of Fred. I was no longer clumsy, and I learned that I really couldn't hurt him. As time went on, Fred and I became best friends. I quickly learned his little quirks and I became confident in him. I also began to talk to him. "Hey, Fred, we're going out to dinner, could you please not gurgle so loud?" In doing this, I accepted Fred and all that he is. I continue to talk to him and prepare him for new experiences. If I'm trying a new food, I let Fred know that "Hey, buddy—tapioca is on the menu—let's see how you do with it." Through my ostomy support group, I've learned to introduce one new food at a time to see what kind of reaction Fred has. If there is a positive reaction, that food goes on my list of foods to eat in the future; if there is a negative reaction—then I don't eat it again.

Throughout this time, I still looked for courage. I read this quote by Thomas Merton: "Courage comes and goes. Hold on for the next supply." I found that very comforting. There were days when I questioned the journey—"Why did this happen to me? What am I supposed to learn from this experience? What is this experience preparing me for?" Many cancer patients ask those questions—they seem to be a part of everyone's journey. Amid the pain, the questions, and the tears, I knew I was growing in my ability to say "yes" to the next part of the journey.

During this time, I discovered the book *Perspective: The Calm Within the Storm* by Robert J. Wicks. This was a very helpful book as I began the healing process. I would slowly read a couple of pages each day. In order to see my growth during the healing process, I had to compare where I was today with where I was yesterday. Sometimes, the growth was so small, it couldn't be seen. It was easy to become discouraged when I couldn't see the growth. Wicks made a suggestion that helped me counteract the discouragement. He suggested making "a list of positive actions—so we can see them as they are: acts of courage." I was physically weak, so there were days when I said, "Catherine, getting up is an act of courage." Another act of courage was to walk fifteen steps further each day. Walking took so much energy and quickly tired me. Changing my wound dressing was painful—yes, there was medicine to take the edge off, but I still viewed it as an act of courage. I became acutely aware of the many acts of courage that filled my day.

Mary's visit with Elizabeth was an act of courage. Courage is born out of vulnerability. Mary went to share her experience of God's presence, knowing that Elizabeth had also experienced God in a special way. Both women said yes not knowing the joys and sorrows that would emerge from it. Our yeses grow and deepen as we continue to examine them. Our acts of courage emerge from our yeses. During our healing process, we need to allow our close friends to see our vulnerability. Dr. P often told me "Catherine, I'm here for you if you want to talk." Having that lifeline made a huge difference. One of the questions I asked Dr. P was, "Why did you put me on a ventilator during surgery?"

"Catherine," he replied, "I didn't know much about your physical condition. I had never met you. I didn't know how strong or weak your systems were. I decided I could easily 'rest' your breathing system so that if one of the other systems got into trouble, your body could send extra energy to the troubled system." Wow, I thought, that's neat.

It's a philosophy that applies to most of life. We allow our close friends to "rest" our troubled spirits, so we can continue to problem-solve. We also share our joys with these friends. Many of my friends' and family's heartfelt visits were acts of courage. It was hard for many people to visit me as I looked so frail and fragile in ICU. Many of them were frightened that I would die; we shared our vulnerability.

One of my most vulnerable times was the Christmas following surgery; I was still receiving chemo treatments and none of us knew whether or not this would be my last Christmas. I wanted to make the "best Christmas memories ever"! So, I decorated the tree, wrapped gifts, and invited friends and family over. I remember unwrapping gifts with a close friend while sharing a glass of wine and remembering our shared Christmases of the past. With tears in my eyes, I said to her, "I want this Christmas to be the best ever, in case I'm not around for the next one."

Writing this book was a huge act of courage; sharing my vulnerability with complete strangers scared me at times. I believe Mary and Elizabeth were vulnerable with each other. I'm sure both of them shared their hopes and dreams for their future children; I'm sure they told and retold their story of the unusualness of their pregnancies; I'm sure they shared their fears of their upcoming childbirths. In the listening and sharing they provided support for each other.

Prayer

Good and gracious God, a small spark lights the darkness. As we heal, keep us aware of the many little visits and acts of kindness from friends and strangers that light our darkness. Help us to embrace acts of courage so that our attitude remains positive and strong. Give us close friends who hold us tight when the tears fall and our courage falters. Remind us that we are strengthened through our vulnerability and that, as Isaiah reminds us, you collect our tears. May our visitations strengthen us as Mary and Elizabeth strengthened each other.

Journal experience

Explain acts of courage to a close friend. Even when we are well, there are many acts of courage in a given day. Agree to track five acts of courage in the next couple of days. Write about them. Share with each other. For me, an act of courage is writing this book.

THE **NATIVITY**

Birthing new, healthy cells

How afraid Mary must have been when she was ready to give birth. As far as we know, no one was with her other than Joseph. Mary knew it was time, and the birth of Jesus brought joy, surprise, and wonder! New life often springs forth in our ordinary daily lives. Perhaps we're working on a long-term project and suddenly there is an inspiration that changes the project's direction. A family moves in next door, and a new friendship is born. Surgery is performed, a hip or knee is replaced, and soon there is a new spring in our step. In one sense, it's difficult to think of cancer cells being killed through chemother-apy as a birthing of new life, yet that is what I believed. I knew all of my cancer cells would die and that the new cells would bring a new cancer-free life.

I still remember when I walked into the cancer center for the first time—the words on the wall, "Cancer Center," kicked me in the gut, and I could feel little tears forming in my eyes. I swallowed those tears and wondered, "What am I doing here?" I still wanted to deny at times that I had cancer. This was a heavy dose of reality. As I sat waiting with one of my religious sisters to meet my oncologist, "Dr. G," I thought about acronyms for the letters.

C = Courage
A = Anger
N = Newness
C = Creative
E = Encouragement
R = Reliable

C = Chemotherapy
E = Embrace
N = Need
T = Tears
E = Emerge
R = Resilience

As I reflected on these words, I saw the need to be emotionally honest. Yes, I was angry; the tears symbolized how frightened I was; I didn't know what to expect. I believed that if I embraced chemotherapy I would have a greater chance of being a survivor. I also knew I was resilient. Throughout my lifetime I was flexible, I adapted to change, I was able to laugh at myself and different situations, I was a problem solver, I loved to set goals, and I was optimistic. A natural part of my personality was quickly finding a silver lining in every cloud! As I looked around the waiting room, I was amazed at the number of people there to see oncologists. The cancer community was so much larger than I anticipated. I wondered if they were as afraid and angry as I was.

Dr. G, the oncologist explained that without chemo my chance of survival was twenty-five percent, and with chemo it was seventy-five percent. I immediately decided that I would receive chemotherapy. I didn't ask my religious community, family, or friends what I should do. It just felt right. I would need twelve chemotherapy treatments, with a treatment every two weeks. A port would be inserted to make it easier to receive the treatments. The oncologist also told me my hair would thin but not totally fall out. Dr. G also mentioned that eighty percent of the people who received this type of chemotherapy responded well. I took a deep breath and knew I would be in that eighty percent! Dr. G was in a hurry to start chemotherapy; he didn't want to wait too long. Chemotherapy slows down the healing process, so he had to wait for the surgical wound to heal. Both Dr. P and Dr. G stayed in close contact with each other so that chemotherapy could begin as soon as I was released by the surgeon.

Once I was released by Dr. P, Dr. G scheduled a time for a port to be inserted. Using a port would make it easier on all of us as I received my twelve chemotherapy treatments. The port was easily inserted and I didn't have any trouble with it. Once again, I felt blessed because I know some cancer patients have a great deal of trouble with their ports.

I started my chemotherapy on September 29, the Feast of Michael, Gabriel, and Raphael. Angels have always been important to me. As a child, I had a special devotion to my guardian angel and often prayed The Guardian Angel Prayer. I was positive the angels would protect me as I gave birth to healthy cells, just as they had protected me throughout my life. I met with Dr. G, who ordered blood work. My blood was healthy, so the nurse accessed my port and then I went to the infusion room to begin the treatment.

My IV pole had a special tag on it so the nurses would know I was receiving my first treatment. The nurses and staff were always very attentive to all the patients, no matter if it were the first treatment or the tenth. They were more than willing to answer questions. I received pre-meds to assist me in tolerating the actual chemo medicines; when the pre-meds were finished, I began the actual chemo. I was usually in the infusion room for about three hours.

The infusion room had many chairs, and soon those of us receiving chemo as well as the nurses, formed a community. We shared our fear, we laughed as we related stories from our week, and we cried as the chemo took its toll at times. Not only were we all birthing new healthy cells, we also birthed a new community. We looked for each other and asked about each other as we continued our treatments. At the end of each treatment, I received a "Chemo-to-go Box" which was attached to me for the next forty-eight hours. It looked like a small black purse, and it slowly delivered the rest of my treatment. When the treatment was finished, the box would beep and one of our nurses would disconnect it. I would then return it to the cancer center so I could use it again in a couple of weeks.

Mary experienced the pains of childbirth, which brought forth new life. She had the support of Joseph throughout the process. Mary had some idea of what to expect, but the reality of the experience is always deeper than the factual knowledge of the experience. Birthing is always a painful process that takes time. It cannot be rushed. Once Jesus was born, Mary most likely quickly forgot the pain of the process and rejoiced over her new son. Joseph, Mary, and Jesus, a family of three, supported each other in the daily ups and downs of life. Joseph and Mary taught Jesus that every transition in life is filled with endings and beginnings.

Prayer

*Good and gracious God, none of us asks for times of
transition. Most of the time, they flow out of current life
experiences: we need a new job because we were laid off;
our company transferred us to a new city; we have a health
issue and need surgery, therapy, etc. We know from past
experiences that even though there are dark moments
within the transitions, there comes a time when light breaks
through and new growth begins. Our awareness deepens,
and the growth is a birthing—a beginning of something
totally new. Remain with us as we wait for the birthing to
happen; give us the courage to stand within the darkness
supporting each other.*

Journal experience

Reflect on the questions: How are your chemotherapy
treatments or your radiation treatments creating new
life in you? How have you formed community with other
cancer patients receiving treatments?

PRESENTATION OF
JESUS IN THE TEMPLE

Allowing others to present our needs to God

M ary and Joseph brought Jesus to the Temple and presented him to God. Simeon and Anna, elderly people who were filled with the Holy Spirit, were sent to meet Jesus. Simeon cradled Jesus in his arms and prayed, "Lord, now let your servant go in peace. Your word has been fulfilled. My own eyes have seen the salvation which you have prepared in the sight of every people. A light to reveal you to the nations and the glory of your people Israel." Jesus was shown to the world, and the world received its mission to reflect God's presence and love. This feast is summed up in three words: encounter, gratitude, and mission.

The Feast of the Presentation has also been known as Candlemas Day. Candles create a warm, reflective, prayerful atmosphere. As a child, I loved going into church and lighting a votive candle as I prayed for different intentions. I believed the candle was similar to a sentinel, standing guard and continuing to present my request to God once I left. Of course, Advent wreath candles were also a favorite— they kept a count of the weeks before Christmas. I loved the Easter vigil—we started in complete darkness and then the fire was blessed and each of us received a light from the Christ Candle—we were being "sent out" to light the world with God's love.

After my diagnosis of Stage III colon cancer, I struggled to pray. I did not have the energy to focus on presenting my needs to God. My body needed all of its energy to begin the physical, mental, and emotional healing process. It was necessary for me to take a medical leave from Blackburn College, where I taught in the education department. One of my first experiences of being prayed for was when the president of Blackburn stopped to visit me in ICU. He brought with him a small stuffed beaver (Blackburn's mascot is Barney Beaver) whose paws were folded. John told me that Barney as well as the entire Blackburn community was praying for my healing. Barney was always within eyesight while I was in the hospital and now graces one of my bookshelves.

Many of my family, friends, and religious community began to pray with and for me throughout my healing process. Old, withered hands folded in prayer asked God to give me the strength needed to heal completely. Young, learning-to-pray hands asked God to heal me so I could play games with them. Folded, middle-aged hands begged God to cure me as I was too young to die. How humbling it was to be on multiple prayer lists and to receive many get-well cards letting me know I was tucked away in everyone's prayers.

Periodically, my own hands folded in prayer as I asked God to bless all of those who took care of me—those who emotionally supported me, those who prayed for me, and those who visited me. Simultaneously, I also believed that those who had gone before me also presented me to God for healing. I was adamant in my belief that my dad, grandparents, aunts, uncles, and some very close friends who had died from cancer also begged God for my complete recovery. But most of my encounters with God at this time were through others. As I chatted with other cancer patients, I found that many of them had the same experience. Praying was difficult, if not impossible, because it was hard to concentrate.

Like Simeon, I was filled with gratitude. I was grateful for my physicians, who were very knowledgeable and filled with compassion. As I continued to heal, I invited them with their families to our motherhouse for Sunday brunch so that not only I but my religious sisters could express our heartfelt gratitude to these two wonderful men. What a joyous occasion it was to share a meal with them and their families as we said "thanks." I was grateful that I was alive and continuing to heal with no complications. I was grateful for the strength that I was finding deep within; yes, there were a few down days but overall, there was a quiet strength.

I began to see a new mission being revealed before me. At first, I wasn't aware of what it was—it emerged as I walked the cancer journey. Family and friends offered to go with me to treatments. I usually told them "Thanks, but I'm OK going alone." A variety of people took turns dropping me off for treatment and picking me up three hours later.

Part of the reason I liked going alone is that it gave me back a bit of my independence, and I also used some of the time for prayer. During treatments, a wonderful woman came around and offered warm blankets. Wrapped in a warm, comforting blanket, I visualized myself wrapped in God's arms. I knew that, no matter the outcome, I deepened my relationship with God in those moments. As I looked around the infusion room, I presented each person I saw to God and asked for his/her healing. I was told that my friendly smile and positive attitude touched many hearts and that other cancer patients looked forward to my presence. Treatment time offered space for praying, reading, visiting, napping, and trusting a little bit more.

Another part of my "new mission" was my deepening ability to listen. In our full-time care facility, as nurses and aides came in to care for me, they often shared joys and hardships; we laughed and looked for ways to ease the challenges. I also brought "new life" to our full-care nursing facility. Many of the retired sisters saw my determination to heal and enjoyed my happy, teasing personality. I began to understand the aging process in a whole new way, and I made some deep and lasting friendships with some of our retired sisters in the ten weeks I lived there. Since I returned to our motherhouse, I have gone to the full-care facility to visit with nurses, aides, and the retired sisters. I'm always welcomed with big grins and hugs. They still cheer me on as I remain on the "maintenance schedule" for cancer checkups.

Together, Mary and Joseph presented Jesus in the temple. He was wrapped in a warm blanket as he was dedicated to God. Simeon and Anna spent years praying in the temple, which developed a contemplative spirit within each of them. As they observed Mary and Joseph presenting Jesus, they recognized him as the Messiah because Simeon and Anna observed not with physical eyes but with contemplative eyes. We too can recognize God's presence in our "mission" if we look at situations with our "heart eyes" and not with our "judgmental eyes." How important it is to trust each other's call to minister to God's people in a variety of ways.

Prayer

Good and gracious God, I quietly come before you. I am filled with gratitude and awe for the many people who are praying for me. I believe in the power of prayer and I know you will hear these prayers. Healing comes in many forms. I accept the healing you choose to send. Perhaps my healing will give me a longer time on earth; perhaps my healing will come in the form of mended relationships; perhaps my healing will come in my ability to forgive someone; perhaps my healing will come through hospice, which leads to eternal healing. I know you love me and know what is best for me at this time. Continue to deepen my trust and allow me to be open to all of the types of healing.

Journal experience

If you have not as yet done so, ask your faith community, family, and friends to pray for your recovery. Describe how it feels to know that you are being prayed for around the clock each and every day.

THE **FINDING** OF **JESUS** IN THE **TEMPLE**

*Experiencing the urgency of life
in grace-filled places*

This mystery begs us to look at the "missing Jesus" from two very different perspectives. First of all, there is the perspective of Jesus. Jesus is in the temple, learning and teaching about God. Jesus has a strong sense of mission at this time. He is listening and responding to God's call to make God known. Jesus also refers to God as "Father," which lets everyone in the temple know he has a family relationship with God and is intimate with God. What part did

Mary and Joseph play in teaching Jesus about God and how to pray? I'm sure they taught him simple prayers at the beginning, and then as he grew older he was trained by rabbis in the art of Jewish prayer. I'm sure Mary and Joseph shared the birth story with Jesus as they continued to model trust, surrender, and faithfulness.

On the other hand, we have Mary's perspective. She is worried about Jesus. Joseph and Mary are entrusted with caring for Jesus and teaching him the life skills necessary for becoming a productive adult. Part of their teaching is to be sure that he develops a relationship with God. Now, Mary feels as though she has erred as a parent—she has lost her child. Frantically, Joseph and Mary search for Jesus. At first, they look for him among family and friends. Often, when children wander away they go to visit family or friends. As the days go by, Mary and Joseph discover Jesus is not with anyone he knows. Eventually, Mary and Joseph find Jesus in the temple. Neither understands why Jesus is there. At the end, Mary "ponders all of these things in her heart." Mary doesn't understand her son and begins to think about who Jesus is and what his mission is. At this point, Mary's yes is built from faithfulness rather than from understanding.

Throughout my cancer journey, a felt presence of God ebbed and flowed. Sometimes, I knew God was close, and I could almost reach out and touch; other times, the darkness seemed overwhelming, and I wondered if God were busy about other business. Mission? What was my mission as I walked this cancer journey? I didn't understand why I had cancer; I continued to wonder what I was being called to do. I remained faithful. I prayed as much as I could; I went to Mass and received communion as often as my energy allowed. I prayed for a deeper trust. I knew "my mission" was evolving because of my new experiences, but I didn't know what it was. I often reflected on Rainer Maria Rilke's words: "Be patient toward all that is unsolved in your heart and try to love the questions themselves, like locked rooms and like books that are now written in a very foreign tongue. Do not now seek the answers, which cannot be given you because you would not be able to live them. And the point is, to live everything. Live the questions now. Perhaps you will then gradually, without noticing it, live along some distant day into the answer." I lived each day waiting, hoping, and being open to the answers I so desperately sought.

As my story spread and friends and family learned that I had come close to death, some of the responses I received were "God has big plans for you." I felt angry each time I heard that response. It seemed to imply that my previous life and ministry weren't important or even enough. It seemed to negate my previous missions. I worked hard to not reply in anger. The other question that brought anger to the fore was "Catherine, are you beating this?" Again, I had to be careful. "Yes, I have cancer; yes, I'm receiving chemotherapy treatments as a curative measure. If God chooses to heal me in different ways and the chemotherapy is not curative, I am not a loser."

I've gained so much from this experience and all my past experiences. There was a very poignant moment in my life in the 1980s that subconsciously shaped many future responses. I was teaching thirty-six second graders. We were watching the launch of the Challenger when it suddenly exploded. There was an uncanny silence in my classroom that was broken as one of my second graders asked, "Sister, if you knew you were going to die, would you have gotten in the spaceship?" There was a deep silence. I knew my response was very important. I replied, "Yes, God only asks us to do two things before we die: 1) allow moms, dads, grandparents, aunts, uncles and friends to love us and 2) to love other people. I know I've done both of those things, so, yes, I would be ready to die." The second grader gave me a smile and answered, "Me, too— I've done those things." Subconsciously, I've carried that belief for many years. I know God is waiting for me with open arms. Deep down, I knew there is nothing I still had to do before I died. I've loved life, people, and God. What more could I want?

As I continued to walk the cancer journey, I found myself searching for a new definition of self, a mission that matched my new experiences and a deeper relationship with God. While searching, I came across the following quote from Terry Hershey: "We are on this journey to name and embrace sanctuaries—places of grace."

A mission that was beginning to emerge for me was to embrace the present. I became deeply aware that there is no guarantee of tomorrow; people who have near-death experiences often end up with a stronger sense of the gift life is. Life is treasured rather than taken for granted. I needed to make sure that I did within each day what I was called to do. There was urgency to life. Part of that urgency encouraged me to look for places of grace each and every day. Sitting in my rocker surrounded in silence with a cup of coffee in hand was a place of grace. Walking with a good friend and sharing hopes, dreams, and frustrations was a place of grace. Realizing without being judgmental that smart phones prevent people from living in the present was a place of grace. Continuing to stay in contact with my surgeon was a place of grace. Grace surrounds us; it's up to us to connect to it through our awareness.

Prayer

Good and gracious God, I praise and thank you for the awareness of the many sanctuaries of grace that surround me. Grace pushes me to search not only for you but for the mission that awaits me as I allow the experiences of being a cancer patient and survivor to touch my deeper self. Give me the patience necessary to not only ask the questions but to live into the answers. Continue to let me feel your presence and know that you walk with me during the frustrating moments when I want to know the answers quickly rather than patiently waiting for the answers to emerge.

Journal experience

Write a dialogue poem between yourself and one of your places of grace. A dialogue poem consists of a conversation between two characters with different perspectives.

Here is a sample:

ROCKING CHAIR   Good Morning, Catherine! I've been waiting for you. Come sit down

CATHERINE   Ah, it's so good to sit and relax. The quiet stills my rushing thoughts.

ROCKING CHAIR   Interesting, I am rocking at breakneck speed; you don't seem very still.

CATHERINE   I've been caught red-handed, my soul wants the quiet but my body is busy rushing ahead of my soul.

THE

SORROWFUL

MYSTERIES

THE **AGONY** IN THE **GARDEN**

Losing the illusion of control

F rom what we read in the Scriptures, Mary was not present for Jesus' agony in the garden. However, mothers have special connections with their children, and I suspect Mary knew from afar that Jesus was struggling. None of us can take away the struggles of another; none of us can fully comprehend the emotional or physical pain of another. Mary supported Jesus from afar. She prayed with and for him as he prepared to once again say yes at a much deeper level.

Part of this mystery is about trust. Does Jesus trust God?

As Jesus grew, did he learn to follow in his mother's footsteps and trust God? It's easy to trust when life is going well. It's easy to say yes when there is no physical or emotional pain. As we look deeper at this mystery, we don't find Jesus saying "I can handle this—let's just do it"; no, we find him praying, "Not my will but yours be done," and being strengthened by an angel. Emotional and physical pain brings with it the promise of God walking with us as we prepare to let go of our own will to follow his. Following God's will is easy when I know and understand the "why," but when the "why" is obscured, then it is more difficult to walk in blind trust.

One of my greatest struggles was losing the illusion of control. My life was centered on doctors' appointments and chemotherapy treatments. The receptionist was able to see all of the doctors' appointments and chemotherapy appointments, so she scheduled future appointments around existing appointments. I never was able to say, "I'm going to a birthday party" or, "I'm planning to visit friends out of town for a few days." My life was totally in the hands of multiple receptionists. There were times when I was scheduled for a chemotherapy treatment but my white blood cell count was too low, so once again the receptionist rescheduled all appointments. Each time this happened, I tried to take a deep breath, relax, and not focus on the disappointment I felt.

Some of the disappointment came from knowing that needing to wait for a treatment prolonged the process. Prolonging the process meant remaining focused on the chemo treatments and not being able to visit out-of-town friends. During this time, I learned to look for a variety of perspectives—if I felt disappointed, I acknowledged the disappointment but looked for a way to think about it differently. I always tried to find the silver lining in the cloud. I learned healing had to be my number one priority and everything else in my life needed to revolve around that priority. Whenever there was a setback from chemotherapy, I eventually learned to view it as a "vacation" that allowed me a "gift of time" to spend however I wanted. I shared this concept with several other cancer patients, and they found it a practical way to cope with the disappointments. After my white cell blood counts were low on two occasions, Dr. G ordered an injection to be given each time I finished a chemotherapy treatment. This injection would encourage the white cells to reproduce. This created more appointments that I needed to work around. While these injections lessened my frustrations about receiving chemo treatments in a timely manner, I was concerned about the expense, even though insurance paid for most of it. This entire process taught me about "letting go."

As I reflected on "letting go," I ran across this quote by Eckhart Tolle: "Stress is caused by being 'here' but wanting to be 'there' or being in the present but wanting to be in the future. It is a split that tears you apart inside." During this time, I became deeply aware that one of the gifts I was receiving was to be present. I needed to take one day at a time and focus on the "now" and not to look forward to the "magic date" when chemotherapy would be finished, or to the CAT scan at the end of chemotherapy that would let everyone know if the treatment was successful. I needed to treasure each moment for what it was. Looking at the "now" helped to lower my expectations, and as I began to do that there was a greater peace with the process. The frustrations were fewer as I grew into acceptance.

I also focused on remembering earlier times of "letting go." Each time I was assigned a new ministry in a new place, I had to let go of friends, programs, and comfort levels. I am a person who roots well wherever I am. I always become actively involved not only in my ministry but also in volunteer work; each move left an emptiness. That emptiness remained until I was rooted in a new place.

When my grandparents, my dad, and friends who had cancer died, I had to let go of significant relationships and look for new ways to remember them as I continued to live. Mary modeled for Jesus how to "let go" many times throughout her life. Mary let go of her preconceived ideas of what her relationship with God should be and accepted the one God offered. She let go of friends and family as she journeyed to Bethlehem, where Jesus was born; and through telling him this story of his birth, she modeled the values necessary for letting go. In searching for Jesus when he was lost, Mary let go of her preconceived ideas of who Jesus was and allowed a new definition of him to emerge.

Each time we let go prepares us for the next time we are called to let go. Letting go is never easy because we always remember the emptiness, the time it takes to establish new relationships, as well as the emotional and psychological energy demanded in times of transition.

Prayer

Good and gracious God, we stand before you with open hands. Give us the grace necessary to allow you to take whatever you want and to bless us with whatever you want us to receive. Help us know that our illusion of control is just that—an illusion. Give us the ability to stand back and trust you to walk with us through emotional and physical pain. Bless the people in our lives who positively model letting go. Give us the courage to share our letting-go moments with others so we can be blessing for each other.

Journal experience

Write a fairy tale in which "letting go" is the theme.

THE **SCOURGING**
AT THE **PILLAR**

*Physical and emotional scars
remind us of our brokenness*

A s I imagine this scene, I see Mary standing nearby. She is horrified by the way her Son is treated; this beating leaves many scars—emotional and physical. Mary continues to pray with and for her Son. Jesus may or may not see his mother, but he senses her presence. None of us can suffer for another or take the suffering away, but we can stand nearby and allow our presence to be our support.

I once heard a story about a small girl sitting on the steps of her home who was crying. Her best friend arrived to play. But when her friend saw her friend crying, she didn't say a word; she just sat down and cried with her.

Just as Jesus had Mary and the women who stood quietly by through his passion, I had several friends who were always there. Like Jesus, I have several physical scars to remind me of the journey I've been on. There is a lengthy vertical scar down my abdomen; I have a permanent stoma, and there is a scar on my upper chest from where a port was put in and removed.

During the healing process of my surgical wound, the nursing staff and aides at our mother house were outstanding cheerleaders who encouraged me to walk to regain my strength and to eat a bit extra to try and put on some of the weight I had lost. At one point, Dr. P, my surgeon, was discussing my weight loss and I quickly said "Well, I'm sure my colon weighed ten pounds, so that's why I'm lighter." Dr. P laughed at me and said "Catherine, your colon did not weigh ten pounds!" "Oh, so what did it weigh?" Lucky for me, he couldn't find the answer in the surgical report.

Rather than sewing my wound closed, I opted for a wound vac (vacuum-assisted closure), and the home health nurse came and changed the dressings. This was a very painful process. The nurse called an hour before she arrived, so our nurses could give me pain medication to help take the edge off. But the wound vac allowed me to heal from the inside out.

I always asked, "Am I healing?" I soon learned that nature healed in its own time. I couldn't eat certain foods or do specific exercises to speed the healing process. I learned how to wait; I experienced Advent in the middle of autumn. The nurse measured the wound each time she came, and little by little the wound began to close. One day, after measuring the wound, the nurse asked "May, I please take a picture of it and send it to your surgeon? I think the wound is healed and the wound vac can be removed." I gave her a big smile and said, "Yes, just don't post my belly on Facebook!" There was lots of rejoicing that day. Each day when I see the scar, I'm reminded of the many people who walked with me throughout this part of the journey.

Fred, my stoma, is a forever reminder of my cancer journey. I am grateful for Fred as he gave me life. Fred and I have our ups and downs. I've learned to eat the foods he tolerates. I've learned how to care for him. I don't ever apologize for Fred if he has an accident or gurgles loudly, I try to handle him as discreetly as possible. My close friends and I celebrate Fred's birthday—there are cards, presents, and his favorite foods. Fred and I continue to correspond with the surgeon who made Fred. Without the surgeon's expertise, I wouldn't be as well as I am today. I learned to accept Fred by treating him as my "other" self. Occasionally, I attend a stoma support group; as I listen to others' experiences, I am deeply grateful that Fred has few issues; others are not so lucky.

My tiniest scar is my port scar. I find that rather interesting, because that scar is a symbol of the longest healing process. I began chemotherapy on September 29 and finished it on March 20. I learned that each of the healing processes had to occur independently. I could not start chemotherapy until the surgical wound was healed. I spent so much of my life before cancer multitasking, and I soon learned in the healing journey that the body's energy needed to be concentrated on a particular area; the queen of multitasking became the princess of single focus.

During this part of the journey, I focused on a thought from Terry Hershey, "To have a future is not about eternity or even our golden years, it is about the permission, the freedom and the persistence to *love* this very day." Throughout the healing process, the message of being present to the "now" was becoming clear. I became more deeply aware of the gifts contained in each day. The presence of family and friends, the nursing staff and aides at our motherhouse, the positive outlook that is a natural part of who I am, learning to wait, and treasuring the natural healing process were gifts that helped me love most days of the journey. The "down days" were those in which I focused on the past—who I was before cancer—or when I focused on the future—how soon can I go back to work? Or when will I gain my weight back? The scars remain, and I treasure the stories they hold and the people I met during this journey. I never thought I would enjoy those memories, but as time has slipped away;

I find myself walking down memory lane and treasuring the gifts I received.

Prayer

Good and Gracious God, our lives are filled with hopes, dreams, and scars. So often, we try to cover our scars; we hide them with clothing or makeup. The scars are symbols of struggle. It is in the process of struggle that we reach for the courage we need to continue. It is in the process of struggle that we ask our friends to stay with us awhile. It is in the process of struggle that we reach out for your hand—a hand that was already there awaiting our grasp. Allow our scars to deepen our trust, keep us from becoming embittered or cynical. Give us the wisdom to know when to share our scars so we can be beacons of hope.

Journal experience

Take time to write a letter to one of your scars.

THE **CROWNING**
WITH **THORNS**

Faithfulness in the midst
of overwhelming suffering

s I continue to reflect on Mary, I can only imagine her pain as she watches her adult child humiliated and mocked. How difficult it was for her to understand the depth of others' cruelty to him. Jesus had already suffered so much, and this incident added more suffering. One of the greatest lessons I learned from Mary was her willingness to accept suffering. Mary showed us that it is possible to watch the suffering and death of her Son and remain faithful. Her tear-stained faithfulness is a gift I clung to when the suffering seemed overwhelming.

Emergency surgery, stage III colon cancer, a stoma, twelve rounds of chemotherapy—wasn't that enough pain and suffering? One would think so, but as with Jesus, there was more to come.

There were seven of us at our motherhouse who were in various stages of chemotherapy and radiation for different types of cancer. We banded together and called ourselves "The Chemo Girls." We laughed together and rejoiced with each other when our blood counts were up. We cried together and shared our disappointment when our blood counts were down or when handfuls of hair began to fall out. We held each other's hands as we pushed food around on our plates, too sick to eat. We shared the names of different medications for nausea our doctors prescribed for us. We walked long halls together and chatted as we tried to keep up or regain our strength. There were late night cups of tea with serious talks about dying—what was it like? There were tears as we examined hope, fear, and love. We asked each other about how one would know when to stop treatments and begin palliative care. We wondered what to say to each other once someone began palliative care. There was presence—big strong hugs and holding onto each other. No words were necessary. Perhaps you have had conversations like these with members of a cancer support group or close friends who have shared this experience.

Slowly, over a period of nine months, five of the seven died. There are two of us remaining. We are the youngest of the group. Both of us have faced the question, "Why are we still here?" Both of us cried buckets of tears as we buried each of the Chemo Girls. Each funeral forced me to step back and revisit hope and reality. Each funeral forced me to integrate faith with hope and reality. Each funeral forced me once again to face my own vulnerability and to continually wonder how I was going to grow strong. I realized the fragility of life, and I was frightened.

Rarely did I share that fear with anyone. Somehow, I always found my next dose of courage when others were around. The paradox of hope and reality was a thinly veiled curtain. How was I going to remain hopeful when I watched courageous women die? Each woman embraced death in her own way. Some were never "ready" to die; they held onto hope as tightly as a child grips his or her teddy bear. Others slowly let go and carefully moved into the active dying process. I often wondered if each person dies the way that she or he lives. If one adjusts quickly and easily to change throughout life, does that person let go more easily? If one slowly let go in various life time experiences, did one slowly let go in the dying process?

As a cancer survivor, I've journeyed into a deeper understanding of loss, grief, hope, acceptance, new life, and reality. In the beginning, I walked in silence and solitude as I tried to integrate my outer experiences with my inner values and faith. Partway through the journey, I realized I could also work on integrating faith and values through sharing with others. We Chemo Girls created sanctuaries for each other. Because of the similarity of our experiences, we didn't often need to use words; a smile, a nod, or a runaway tear spoke volumes. Terry Hershey affirmed our experiences when he wrote, "When we create sanctuaries, we are creating places of healing. We are making space to see and be seen. To give wholeheartedly, to offer comfort, or reprieve, or hope."

Mary was a place of healing for Jesus. She gave wholeheartedly; she held nothing back. I'm sure she wanted her Son to follow in Joseph's footsteps—to be an ordinary carpenter. When her Son began his ministry, she didn't tell him not to follow his call. She supported him, listening to him as he preached. Mary offered comfort. Her silent, loving presence during the entire crucifixion process provided Jesus continued comfort and hope.

Most cancer patients have friends or family who are places of healing. As cancer patients share their struggles and hopes, someone is there to affirm, encourage, or just be present while gently holding the story. Each of the Chemo Girls became a place of healing for each other. We were honest with each other—we gave wholeheartedly—we laughed, cried, and hoped together. We comforted each other. We intuitively knew when to challenge each other to "get up and keep going" and when to "move into palliative care." We learned that "healing" has many different faces and that each face provides opportunities.

Prayer

Good and gracious God, may our lives be filled with moments in which we choose to give wholeheartedly to those who cross our path. Deepen our awareness of those who need a friendly smile, a hand to hold, or a quiet presence. Allow our journey to bring comfort and hope to those who are discouraged or to those who have lost hope. May the healing we experience be a light for those who wait to be healed, and may we have the courage to share our journey so others may receive the gift of faithfulness born from pain and suffering.

Journal experience

Write a letter to a friend, explaining how you have given wholeheartedly.

JESUS CARRIES
THE CROSS

*Learning to balance carrying
the cross alone with asking for
help in carrying the cross*

Mary silently walks and watches as Jesus carries his cross. During part of this journey, Jesus shoulders his cross alone. He stumbles, falls, rises, and continues his walk to the crucifixion site. At one point in the journey, Simon of Cyrene is forced to help Jesus carry his cross. I'm sure Mary wanted to reach out and help him bear the weight of the cross. No mother wants to see a child suffer; no mother wants to bury a child. Mary's strong courageous presence strengthened Jesus and helped him remember the love the Father has for him.

One of a mother's greatest gifts is to help us remember. As a child, I listened to my mom tell stories about my baptism and my siblings' baptisms. She shared stories of when we were growing up that were funny, serious, irritating, and filled with love, and it was in the remembering that I re-experienced the love God has for all of us.

As we look at the crosses we carry, sometimes we choose to carry them alone, and at other times, we choose to have someone assist us. There are moments when we are strong and can shift the cross from one position to another; there are moments when the suffering is tough and we need a respite so we can continue the journey. It took me awhile to learn that it was ok to ask for help; many cancer patients hesitate to ask for help: none of us wants to be a burden. We also want to protect our family and friends: we don't want them to see us ill; we don't want them to worry about us. How important it is to allow others to gift us with their help. Family and friends feel so helpless; I quickly learned that allowing them to help in small ways was a gift I could give. At times, I swallowed my "independence" just to allow someone to feel needed.

One of the drugs I received during chemotherapy was oxaliplatin; the worst side effect was a sensitivity to cold. I couldn't touch anything in the refrigerator without using oven mitts, and all of my food and drink had to be either room temperature or warmer. This was very difficult for me because I love icy cold drinks. The first couple of times that I forgot and touched something cold, I received a lasting shock. It didn't take me long to remember! Space heaters became my best friends! I told my oncologist, "There ought to be a law against using oxaliplatin during an Illinois winter." We both chuckled.

It was during the tenth treatment that suddenly I had an anaphylactic reaction to oxaliplatin. I couldn't breathe, my heart started racing, and I turned a bright Christmas red and began to break out in a rash. The nurses immediately stopped my treatment, hooked me up to monitors, and called my doctor, who came immediately. The nurses began flushing my lines and administering drugs the doctor quickly ordered.

None of my friends or family was present for this medical emergency. I was afraid; I wanted someone to hold my hand and reassure me. The doctor and nurses were too busy watching the monitors and providing different drugs to counteract the reaction. Once the drugs began to take effect, my symptoms began to dissipate. At one point, my doctor said, "Catherine, you're going to be all right; the numbers on the monitors are looking better." I replied, "I think the numbers are lying, I'm not feeling very all right." The doctor smiled at me and said, "It will be awhile before you feel all right, but we are headed in the right direction." After this treatment, I went home and slept for five hours.

There were many friends who helped me carry this cross. While I was in the Intensive Care Unit, I received many cards. One of the nurses who brought the cards into me each day always said, "Look how much you are loved." That simple phrase spurred me on as I began the healing process. One friend came every Saturday to visit and eat lunch with me. How I looked forward to those visits!

One Saturday, when my friend arrived, I was up and dressed and had purse in hand and announced we were going to Walmart to buy sweat pants (my regular pants made my surgical wound ache), and then we were going to Washington Park to the art show. She hesitated a bit; she wasn't sure she wanted to be responsible for my first outing. She saw the determined look in my eyes and decided not to argue. Off we went! As I slowly led her through unknown parts of our motherhouse, she realized that no one knew that I was planning to go out! After the shopping expedition, I said to her, "I think I need to go home. I don't have any energy left." But how good it was to go out just for a bit.

Another friend took me to the public library every other week, and we would stop for coffee. I walked very slowly, and she had to carry my books. It was a short outing, but again it helped build my strength. Another friend made sure I had fresh flowers every week; the beauty those provided along with her visit made the cross lighter. Another friend stopped in to pray with me each evening just before I went to sleep. There are countless other examples of people who were willing to help me carry this cross.

One of the gifts of this journey was finding the balance of carrying my cross alone or asking for someone to help me. This gift continues to be used today. Our lives are filled with a variety of crosses; we must continually strive to create a balance of walking alone or walking with someone.

Prayer

Good and gracious God, give us the wisdom to know when to carry our crosses alone and when to ask for help. Bless those who help us in a special way. Give them the gentleness needed to lift our crosses. Give us the ability to walk with someone and not push him/her away because "we want to be brave." Help us be aware of the many gifts that those who help us give to us. Help us treasure the time spent with friends during our healing process.

Journal experience

Write a Diamante (poetry form) about your cross

LINE 1:   Noun or subject: one word

LINE 2:   Two adjectives that describe Line 1

LINE 3:   Three "ing" words that describe Line 1

LINE 4:   Four nouns—the first two are connected
with Line 1; the last two are connected with Line 7

LINE 5:   Three "ing" words that describe Line 7

LINE 6:   Two adjectives that describe Line 7

LINE 7:   Noun synonym for the subject

THE **CRUCIFIXION**

*The beginning of
the transition from cancer patient
to cancer survivor*

S o few details, yet we know that Mary stood at the foot of the cross with the beloved disciple and other women. Mary witnessed the entire way of the cross. Now, she stands at the foot of the cross. I wonder, did she reflect on the different incidents in Jesus' ministry and how his deep love for God brought him to this point? Did she reflect on the times he healed others and gave them a relationship with God based on the "spirit of the law" rather than the "letter of the law"? Did she reflect on the first "yes" she uttered and how her Son learned from her "yes"?

Jesus looked at Mary from the cross. Did he see the pain and suffering in her eyes? Did he wish he could have spared his mother this terrible experience? Amidst the pain and suffering, I'm sure there was deep love and understanding. I'm sure Mary's cheeks were tear-stained; tears are a sign that we love something or someone very much.

Together, Mary and Jesus experienced darkness. Jesus prepared to surrender to death, and Mary continued her life of surrender that began with the Annunciation. Mary's life was filled with moments of surrender. Each experience of surrender prepared her for the next moment. I imagine that Jesus silently watched his mother surrender time and time again, and through her modeling he was able to open himself to the final surrender of death.

In earlier reflections, I mentioned there were several deaths throughout this journey. First, I learned how to be ill; it was difficult to not be able physically to maintain my usual full schedule. Second, sometimes little things became big things because I had so little I could control. I remember a meltdown over mashed potatoes; I was hungry, and all I wanted was a bowl of mashed potatoes, which couldn't be found! Third, I had to learn to accept Fred, my stoma, and the many ways he changed my life. Fourth, during chemotherapy treatments there were a few weeks in which my white blood count was very low and I couldn't receive treatments and I was so tired. I was tired of being tired!

Another small death occurred after the completion of chemo. Throughout the chemo process, Dr. G, the oncologist, always asked if I had any numbness or tingling in my fingers or toes from medicine side effects. I was always able to shake my head and say no. But then the tingling began when my treatments were finished. This happens to about twenty percent of the patients who receive the type of therapy I did. They told me there is a small chance that it would subside after a year. Unfortunately for me, this has not happened. For the most part, it does not affect my ability to do what I want to do; it's just annoying.

A darkness that surprised me was the transition from cancer patient to cancer survivor. Most cancer patients look forward to the day when treatments are finished. My hair had thinned, and my beautician had found a new hair style for me that allowed my limp hair to look becoming. My nails were soft and tore easily. I was eager to have my hair and nails return to their normal states. Upon arriving for my final treatment, the usual blood tests were done and, once again, my white blood cell count was borderline. My compassionate oncologist said, "It's OK, Catherine, I'm not going to keep you from your last treatment." He talked with me about the protocol he designed for continued checkups. I would have blood drawn every three months for a Cancer Marker Test, and a CAT scan every six months.

As time went on, the time between these tests would lengthen. I realized I would miss the friends in the infusion room and the routine of seeing the oncologist every other week, which was a safety net. Now I had to create new safety nets; I had to let go of the comforting routine. This transition was the final death of the cancer patient journey. I said goodbye to the nurses, the patients who were finishing their treatments, and my oncologist; I took a deep breath and smiled as I waved and then said, "See you in three months." I was surprised by the tiny tears that filled my eyes. I was excited that the chemotherapy was completed, but I was frightened because I didn't know what to expect during the transition. I was afraid the cancer would recur; I was afraid my energy level wasn't the same as it was before the illness; I was afraid that I would be defined only as a cancer survivor, and I am so much more than that! In talking with other cancer patients, I learned my fears were very typical and that many medical communities need to improve the support they offer patients as we transition from patient to survivor. Doctors and nurses rarely tell us what to expect or share resources of where we can find support if we feel we need assistance.

During this entire journey, I stayed at our motherhouse so I had the support of the nursing staff and the retired sisters, who were wonderful cheerleaders and pray-ers! Now, I was ready to move back to where I had been living before I became ill. This transition came quicker than anyone anticipated: just ten weeks after surgery. I was strong enough to return home. I lived alone, so not only was I going to have to readjust to my physical surroundings; I would need to readjust my expectations for support.

Suddenly, I didn't feel very confident. What happens if Fred and I get into trouble? Who's close by to help? These questions darted in and out of my consciousness on a frequent basis. I packed my belongings and prepared to leave. Once again, saying goodbye was difficult. On the other hand, I was ready to return to my normal routine. One of my good friends went grocery shopping with me and then followed me as I drove home. She helped me unpack the groceries and settle in, and then she gave me a hug and away she went. How strange it felt to be home!

Returning home was like walking into a time capsule. I had left hurriedly to go to the emergency room and thought I'd be back in a few hours—which turned into a few months. My bed was unmade; there was laundry waiting and dusting and vacuuming to be done. I slowly started to put the house in order. Vacuuming was not on my "to do" list, so I called a friend and arranged a time when she could vacuum for me. I had to do tasks in small spurts; my energy was returning, but it wasn't one hundred percent.

I realized that I would need to pace myself. I was still healing and could easily become exhausted. I also lowered my expectations of what needed to be done as far as housework was concerned. Dusting and vacuuming did not have to be every-week occurrences. I love to cook, but I cooked several entrees at a time and then reheated them. Naps after work became acceptable for a few weeks. The readjustment took longer than I anticipated. I was grateful that my friends trusted my "good sense" and did not continually check in to see how I was doing. There was a fine line between being "independent" and being "supported." I had promised many of them that if I needed something, I would let them know.

Part of this dying was also being deeply aware that the cancer journey changed me. I would never be the same as I was before. At this point, I couldn't "define" the new me; I intuitively knew that new values would emerge and that I needed to grieve the self that had died. Because I am an introvert, it would take many months for me to examine and reexamine the experiences and begin to integrate them so the new self could emerge.

Prayer

Good and gracious God, our lives are filled with small dying moments. Sometimes these moments come during transitions; sometimes they come as we let go of previous routines; sometimes they come as we experience loneliness and fear. Give us the grace to keep our hands open so new growth can begin from these small deaths. Grant us courage so we can share our experiences with others and allow them to support us with encouragement and hugs. Remind us that Mary supported Jesus throughout his suffering and pain; help us realize that we never have to walk alone.

Journal experience

Reflect on the many times you have allowed others to gift you with their presence as you prepared for a new experience.

THE

GLORIOUS

MYSTERIES

THE **RESURRECTION**

Moments filled with new life

T he Scriptures do not tell us where Mary was when she met her resurrected Son. What a glorious meeting it was! I imagine big, tight hugs in which neither one wanted to let go of the other. I imagine Jesus and Mary sitting together remembering and reexamining all of Jesus' teachings, his miracles, and their relationships with everyone, and how both of them continued to surrender to God's will while maintaining hope.

Resurrection begins the moment the stone is rolled away from the tomb. Dying is necessary to understand the future. We walk away from what sustained us in the past. Suffering is not something we ever let go of—it becomes a part of who we are. Total surrender is the preparation for resurrection.

There was a time in my life when I believed resurrection happened all at once. As I've grown older, I realize that resurrection is much like dying—it happens little by little. There seems to be a time of "suspension"; I've totally surrendered and death has occurred, but there's an "unknowing" of what will follow. I think of suspension as the moment in the trapeze artist's performance when she has let go of the one trapeze and is reaching for the new trapeze and is suspended in midair until the new trapeze arrives. At that moment all she can do is trust. Both dying and resurrection take courage. We are never sure of the "wait time" between the two events.

My first moment of resurrection was returning to work. Colleagues and friends continued to support me as I began to embrace a full-time work schedule. It was so good to return to routine; it was so good to once again focus on students, committee meetings, etc., even though I needed to continue chemotherapy treatments. Everyone welcomed me back; all of us were eager to resume some sort of normalcy.

I had been able to arrange to receive chemotherapy on the weekends. I spent every other Friday morning in the infusion room, and then I received a "to-go box" of chemotherapy that I finished on Sunday morning. I made sure to clear my calendar for these weekends as I knew I would need extra rest. Once again, I didn't have to worry about who would care for me if I became ill during these treatments; I spent these weekends at our motherhouse. It was good to see the sisters and to allow them to support me. I realize other cancer patients do not always have a strong support system and worry about being cared for if they become ill during continued treatments.

The next resurrection moment arrived when I finished my chemotherapy. I mentioned earlier that this was difficult, but at the same time it was a relief! I had to wait three months before Dr. G, the oncologist, could do a Cancer Marker Test; this would determine if the chemotherapy had been effective. Waiting was difficult. I continued to visualize healthy cells replacing cancerous cells. Finally, the day arrived! I had my first blood test and the results were all that I hoped for! The chemotherapy worked and there were very few cancer cells present. There was great rejoicing among family and friends.

To this day, my blood work and CAT scans are good; I am a cancer survivor! Not everyone is blessed with this good news. Presently, I have blood work done every six months and a CAT scan once a year. When the time nears for these tests, I find myself pacing the floor and wondering if the news will continue to be good. I know deep down, that if the news isn't good, there are options to consider and that God is with me as I make choices. Often, death and resurrection moments are two sides of the same coin. It's up to us to decide on which side to focus.

Another resurrection moment arrived as I realized that I had totally adjusted to my stoma, Fred. Taking care of him is so natural that I rarely think about him. Just as a mom takes a diaper bag with her for her little one, I have a "Fred" bag filled with supplies for emergencies that I take with me. I talk to Fred and prepare him for new experiences; the first time we flew, I explained to him that we might have to explain his presence to the TSA, and that the cabin pressure might bother him; however, but Fred handled his first flight very well. Afterward, he said, "Hey, Catherine—now you can call me 'Flying Fred!'"

The biggest moment of resurrection occurred as I was offered a new position at Marian University exactly at the same time and on the first anniversary of the day I had been rushed to emergency surgery with my life hanging in the balance. In my new position, I teach both undergraduate and graduate students, and I also learned to teach online. This was a wonderful professional move. I have grown so much and enjoy the new challenges this position gives me. My energy level is high, and none of my new colleagues knows my story. I did not allow my cancer journey to define what I could or couldn't do.

A surprising resurrection moment happened one day when I was in a hospital room with my mom, who had fallen; the nurse who entered her room to ask the typical admittance questions kept staring at me, and I found myself staring back. Eventually, we said to each other, "It seems like I know you." Simultaneously, we both realized that she had cared for me when I was in ICU. She was amazed and excited to see how good I looked and how much energy I had.

Other resurrection moments come when I am ready to share my story and allow it to help others who are walking a similar journey and need a helping hand as they struggle to find answers to so many questions or to deepen their faith. I am a very private person; in fact, when I was first hospitalized our prioress general asked if she could e-mail our community and ask them to pray for me. I emphatically said no. She pushed a bit and said, "I'll just tell them you are hospitalized without sharing the details." So, I gave her a hesitant yes. As time passed, I realized that I needed to share how walking in Mary's footsteps helped me along the way. I believe that if these reflections help just one person, the purpose for writing this book is fulfilled. I also know there are more resurrection moments to come; I don't know what these moments will be, but I know I need to be aware of and open to them when they emerge.

Prayer

*Good and gracious God, help us look for the resurrection
moments that flow out of death. Give us the patience
needed as we wait for resurrection to occur. Give us the
grace needed to celebrate resurrection moments. Help us
understand that sometimes our resurrection moments are
small when we are hoping for a "big resurrection." Never
let us lose hope, and remind us that you are with us as we
watch and wait for the stone to be rolled away.*

Journal experience

Reflect on how death and resurrection moments have
impacted your life. How have these moments transformed you?

ASCENSION

Bridging between
"my old self" and "my new self"

T he gospel writers give so little information about the time between the
resurrection and the ascension. Forty
days is a long time; I imagine Jesus,
the disciples, Mary, and so many
others used this gift of time to savor,
to remember, and to prepare to say goodbye. Jesus probably
spent time telling everyone that part of his mission was to
return to the Father while simultaneously preparing everyone to go out and share the message he taught. One of the
ascension's themes is to see everything as undeserved gift,
to stand with open hands allowing God to put new experi-

ences in our hands and to take out gifts that are no longer needed. Learning not to cling to what we have is a lesson that is repeated over and over in our lifetime.

Throughout life, we create many relationships. Some relationships are filled with deep love, while other relationships are merely acquaintances. Sometimes, we find employment that deeply fulfills us and we commit ourselves to it wholeheartedly, while at other times, employment is merely a job that keeps us afloat. Our grief is greater during losses that were built on a deep and lasting love. I wonder, "How do I survive without that person's physical presence?" or "How do I survive being laid off when I was totally committed and energized by the work I did?"

As a cancer survivor I found there were moments when I missed my old self. There was a time when I loved to see how many meetings, activities, etc., I could schedule in one day; I ran through days rather than walking through them. I multitasked over and over—not really being fully present to what I was doing but accomplishing a great deal. I could jump in the car and take long trips without being concerned about when I ate or what I ate. I wasn't afraid that cancer would return or that my friends might die. I didn't become irritated with people who always focused on the future while ignoring the present and the many gifts contained within it.

As much as I missed my old self, I knew that the resurrection moments were preparing me for a new mission. I was aware that, once I became comfortable with my new self, I would automatically respond from these deeper values through both word and action. To become comfortable with the new self, I had to gently hold the old self, thank it for the gifts it gave me, and acknowledge the grief that settled in my soul while waiting for my new self to emerge.

Every experience we have becomes a part of who we are. We never totally forget people who loved us or whom we loved, even though they may not be physically present. We never forget the road we traveled with grief-filled eyes and hearts. These moments are forever engraved in our memories. These memories are the building blocks between our old self and the emerging new self.

This also opened a door in understanding the ascension at a deeper level. I know that Jesus spent many hours helping his mother and his friends begin to build a bridge between his physical presence and the "Spirit" that would descend after he left. Jesus knew everyone would grieve the lack of his physical presence but he was careful to explain that he would be with them in a new and different way. Mary and the Apostles had to stand with open hands and hearts as they grieved what they once knew and allowed it to become a part of a new way of relating to Jesus.

Throughout this experience, I learned not to ask "why?" At this time, there is no answer. One of the doctors who carefully examined my pre-cancer medical records said, "Catherine, you are a statistical anomaly; there is absolutely nothing to indicate you would ever be diagnosed with colon cancer."

One of my new ways of relating to Jesus is through a deeper awareness of those who struggle with cancer. I had heard about people who had cancer, but I never really understood the depth of their experiences. As I grocery shopped or ate in restaurants, I became very aware of cancer patients; they were easy to spot with turbans wrapped around their heads or a pale color or sometimes overly bright eyes from the steroids received as premedication for chemo treatments. I quietly said "hello" to each of them. Once I was away from them, I would utter a prayer for them and their families.

Another "new" way of relating to Jesus is that I am able once again to focus on my prayer and to meditate for longer periods of time. I knew from lots of spiritual reading that Jesus promised to be with us in suffering, but now I know from experience that Jesus is with *me* in suffering. I experienced the ebb and flow of his closeness throughout this journey. Often Jesus is with us through others. At times, I need to step back and remember that all of us carry Jesus within, and when I ask if you need help, it is Jesus asking.

As I have continued to embrace life with all that it holds, I do so now with physical scars, a stoma, a deeper sense of life's fragility, and a stronger compassion for all who suffer. On many days, I seem to radiate an inner peace of which I am unaware that was born through suffering. Strangers approach me and often share their sufferings; others seem to sense a deep compassion. Yes, I dance through most days; and even though at times my dance is tentative because I still get frightened, I know that my dance is beautiful and that as God watches from the "balcony," God thinks "This is my beloved daughter in whom I am well pleased."

Prayer

Good and gracious God, our lives are filled with moments of dying, rising, and ascending. Help us realize that you are present with us in a variety of ways. Help us carefully hold our old selves, treasuring the many gifts that bless our lives. Grace us with the ability to envision the new gifts born from the old gifts. Give us the courage necessary to stay with our grief until it calls us to dance.

Journal Experience

Create two or three haikus about grief. Remember a haiku consists of three lines. The first line has five syllables, the second line has seven syllables, and the third line has five syllables.

Here is a sample:

> *Grief poured out of me*
> *An angry, rushing blue stream*
> *Desiring stillness*

DESCENT OF
THE **HOLY SPIRIT**

Responding to God's Spirit

M ary and the disciples were filled with grief after the ascension. I imagine they went about their ordinary, daily lives with heavy hearts and then gathered in the evenings to remember and share their memories. I imagine that they also wondered, "What are we to do now?" Our friend and leader is gone, and we are afraid." It was probably during one of these evenings that they suddenly heard the rush of the wind and saw the tongues of fire over each other's heads while experiencing the Spirit of God in a deeper way.

This experience of the Spirit transformed them from fearful, hidden persons to bold, enthusiastic, hope-filled persons. The Apostles and Mary were no longer weak and discouraged; they were aware of the dynamic power of love, and they were inspired to live and teach the messages Jesus taught them.

Within our lives there are many Pentecost moments— moments when we hear the Spirit or feel the Spirit nudge us into transforming moments or deeper growth. It is up to us to listen for these moments and to follow through on the nudges we receive. Most of the time, these moments are unpredictable and unexpected. We are surprised by the Spirit at work in our lives. The Spirit works in two distinct ways. At times we are "filled" with the Spirit, and at other times we are "led" by the Spirit. Sometimes, these ways are very distinct and we can label the experience as one or the other, but sometimes these ways are intertwined and it's hard to distinguish them. The awareness of the Spirit at work is more important than the label we attach. All of our Pentecost moments are rooted in love and compel us to share the love we received.

Recently, I was talking with a complete stranger about health insurance and the different types of coverage. Usually, I am a very private person and I don't share the fact that I am a colon cancer survivor with a stoma. For some reason, I felt the nudging of the Spirit, and I told him about my cancer. He looked at me and said, "I also don't have a colon. I have a J pouch that is causing trouble. Could we chat a bit about your experience?" We both felt very comfortable continuing this conversation. This opened the door for future conversations. He is having surgery in the near future to discard the J pouch and return to a permanent stoma. Through the Spirit's lead, I can support him as I share products that help me care for "Fred" as well as share my story of how I had a few meltdowns and then learned how to accept "Fred."

A friend from whom I hadn't heard in over a year contacted me recently. He had a liver transplant at the same time I had surgery. He's doing very well with the transplant, but is facing colon surgery due to ulcerative colitis. He was unaware that I had a stoma but was inquiring about the colon surgery. He was frustrated and angry. "Catherine," he said, "I just want a break." I can easily empathize with him. Experiencing medical issue after medical issue leaves one searching for deeper answers. Once again, I was totally honest with him and shared the ins and outs of colon surgery and the adjustment period with a stoma. He was very surprised to learn of my stoma. "I had no idea," he said. "You were attractively dressed; there was no hint of a 'Fred.'" I promised him continued prayers and asked him to stay in touch.

While I was on retreat last summer, I began rereading my journal and relooking at the art I had done while I was recovering from surgery and chemotherapy. I suddenly heard the

Spirit whisper that I needed to take my notes and give them form. I must admit, I tried to ignore the Spirit's prompting for a few days, but then I realized I needed to begin to tell the story and look at it from a variety of perspectives. This prompting of the Spirit led me to a deeper acceptance of my cancer journey. Later on, I stopped by my surgeon's office to visit with him for a few moments and I heard myself say, "If anyone is struggling with accepting his or her stoma, please have this person contact me, I'd be happy to share my journey." This is a whole new part of me.

The Spirit leads me to be more compassionate. I understand in a much deeper way there are many losses in everyone's life. All losses demand time to heal; all losses must be embraced at different levels; all losses distract us and keep us from focusing. Allowing people to share their stories of loss helps them to begin to make sense of the loss. I am a college professor; many of my students experience the death of grandparents, a breakup with significant others, parental divorce, and loss of jobs. With the prompting of the Spirit, I invite students to share their stories with me. When I know that a student isn't able to focus, I allow them extra time for assignments.

At other times, the Spirit leads my restless, worried heart to walk along the lake and embrace the beauty of the trees, the sparkling water, and the warm sun. Such an experience provides stillness, solace, and a deep presence of God.

I was filled with the Spirit of joy and peace as I moved

to a new job in Wisconsin. I found an oncologist and a primary physician who were willing to walk the cancer maintenance journey with me. I trust both of them and have grown to appreciate their compassion and care. My new position professionally challenges me, and it is a very life-giving experience.

Another experience of being filled with the Spirit of wonder and awe came as I was reading *The Gene* by Siddhartha Mukherjee. I suddenly realized how physically complex we are as human beings and how our genes and the human genome are reflections of the God who made us. Genetic research offers so many possibilities as researchers continue to look for cancer cures.

We always have a choice on whether or not to respond to the Spirit's nudging. The Spirit will always lead us to a deeper love of God and to a deeper love of those with whom we come in contact. Each day, we need to reflect on the evidence of where we did or did not turn toward love. As we walk through our days, are we aware of the Spirit asking us to help someone in distress? Are we aware of tears born out of compassion when we listen to someone's loss? Are we aware that only our presence is needed and words might destroy someone's growth? May we look and listen for the Spirit, who propels us to be the hands and feet of Jesus.

Prayer

Good and gracious God, help us to recognize Pentecost moments. You call us to share your deep love with everyone we meet. Transformation demands courage. Give us the courage to step outside our usual boundaries and embrace people in need of hope. Help us be the hands and feet of Jesus even when we are tired or not in the mood to reach out to others. Deepen our awareness of the Spirit within who begs to be shared.

Journal experience

Create a litany of gratitude for the moments you have been surprised by the Spirit.

ASSUMPTION OF MARY INTO HEAVEN

Present and future hope-filled moments

Scripture tells us so little of what happened between the descent of the Holy Spirit and the Assumption. I believe the Apostles and Mary went about their daily tasks filled with a deeper understanding of their call to share in the message and mission of Jesus.

As I reflect on the Assumption, I am struck by two thoughts. First, Mary's experience gives me hope that there is a life beyond this one. This mystery deepens our faith in the communion of the saints. And second, we are native to two places: heaven and earth. At times, we grow so accustomed to our earthly journey that we forget we are pilgrims on the way to eternity. When we die, we leave behind our comfortable sweaters, our homes that are safe havens, the relationships we cultivated, and all that is familiar. We spend so much of our life divided—wanting to achieve success, wanting to grow professionally, while simultaneously wanting to walk in the footsteps of Jesus, Mary, and all the saints. Often there is a tension between these values; we make choices. We live in hope that at the moment of death, the fullness of life will fill our soul, and God will welcome us home, saying, "This is my beloved, in whom I am well pleased." We will live an undivided life focused on the eternal presence of God.

As I continue my cancer journey, and as I have met other cancer patients and survivors, I have come to realize that this group of people and their support groups constantly straddle heaven and earth. On one hand, most people are filled with hope that the doctors will achieve a cure or that there will be a period of remission. People write "bucket lists" of places to go, people to meet, or longed-for experiences. There are cancer patients who willingly participate in cancer research studies hoping that the treatments they receive will prolong their lives and/or provide future cancer patients with new cures and new hope. Many of these patients, their families, and their friends also participate in marathons, walks, etc., that raise money for cancer research.

There are online support groups that provide knowledge, compassion, and hope.

On the other hand, there are days that include a longing for eternity. Being filled with God's presence in small ways creates a hunger for God's eternal presence. At points, the chemo or radiation takes a heavy toll and hope is low; giving up looks attractive. Caregivers become exhausted and can only see their loved ones suffering and wonder at times how much more everyone can take. Many cancer patients have an innate sense as to when it is time to begin palliative care. Hospice or home hospice begins to help patients and their families prepare for the final leg of the journey. Compassionate hands and hearts offer gentle care during the final dying process.

One of my favorite prayer forms is to imagine myself in one of the gospel scenes. And on All Saints Day, I imagined myself in heaven walking and talking with various saints. I imagined spending time with St. Catherine of Siena, who was a strong and courageous woman, or with St. Thomas Aquinas, who was a very learned man. He believed that we are like library books on loan from God to earth and each other, and that eventually our "due date" is up and we return to heaven. I also walked and talked with my dad, my grandparents, and other "friends" who are enjoying eternity. My belief in the communion of saints became much stronger. Not only did I have people on earth praying for me, but I knew my dad, my grandparents, and several "best friends" were also watching over me from heaven. During one of my prayer periods, I created a litany of all of my heavenly pray-ers. It was a wonderful way to reconnect with a few people I had forgotten.

The second thought that has held my attention is that God lifted Mary to God's self and that I can share in this by lifting others up to God. I do this through prayer and service. Many times, we offer to pray for one another. Sometimes it's because of a crisis; sometimes it's a prayer filled with gratitude for gifts received. At other times, different people ask us to pray for them. There are times in our lives when we are incapable of praying: our faith is weak, or physical or emotional pain prevents us from being able to still the soul as we try to lift our hearts to God. How humbling it was to be on so many prayer lists. What a grace it was to hear people say, "I'm praying for you."

It was toward the end of my chemotherapy treatments that I had a spiritual experience that left a strong mark on my soul. I knew that all of my religious community prayed for me throughout this cancer journey. I was at our motherhouse for a meeting, and part of the schedule included Mass. One of the sisters asked if I would help distribute Communion. I quickly said yes. While I was giving out Communion, I realized that these very hands in which I was placing the Body of Jesus had lifted me up in prayer, and now I was able to give them the Body of Jesus. Tears rolled down my cheeks as I realized at a deep level how connected we are in the body of Christ. There is an ebb and flow within the body of Christ, and no matter how weak or how strong we are, we are called to either give or receive; and this can only be accomplished if we stand with open hands, realizing that we have done nothing to earn the gifts we give each other.

Some of these gifts come through serving others. We take time to volunteer at a school, hospital, or parish, and we meet a variety of needs. At other times, we serve through donating gently used items and/or money to Goodwill, Catholic Charities, or the Salvation Army. Within our families, we serve each other by taking on an extra task so our significant other can get away. We quietly stand by while our spouse is ill; we spend extra time just being present. The Spirit expands our love as we continue to straddle heaven and earth.

Prayer

Good and gracious God, we are pilgrims on the way to eternity. Help us realize that not only are we supported on our journey by family and friends, but that we are also connected with the communion of saints. Deepen our hope during the dark moments, and help us accept and embrace our longing for eternity. May we find peace as we live in the tension of belonging to two places—heaven and earth.

Journal Experience

Create a bucket list for earth and a bucket list for heaven.

THE **CORONATION** OF **MARY AS QUEEN** OF **HEAVEN** AND **EARTH**

Examining the jewels in Mary's crown

I n reflecting on this mystery, I often look at the jewels in Mary's crown. For me, her jewels consist of waiting, surrender, suffering, faithfulness, and love. Each of these jewels reflects Mary's relationship with God as well as her relationships with those with whom she walked.

Mary spent much of her life *waiting*. She waited nine months for Jesus to be born; during those nine months, she fed and nourished, guarded and protected Jesus. Mary was very aware that Jesus was growing within her. Mary waited with Elizabeth for John to be born. When Jesus was lost as she and Joseph were returning home, Mary waited with an anxious heart, wondering how she could lose someone who was entrusted to her care. Mary didn't have Jesus nor could she hold him, she waited in emptiness as the search continued.

As cancer patients and survivors, we wait. We wait for healing from surgery so we can begin chemotherapy and/or radiation treatments. We wait for blood work and scans to be returned, holding our breath hoping for good news. We wait for hair to grow back or return to its normal consistency. We wait for weight to return. We wait for side effects from medicines to subside or at least abate. We wait for new selves to be born as we grieve the death of our old self. We wait with other cancer patients. We wait with Mary.

Waiting often leads to *surrender*. As Mary waited, she began to pray as her Son did: "Not my will, but your will be done." Mary knew God had a plan, a plan that was filled with mystery. This plan would unfold little by little; Mary couldn't see the "big" plan; she had to walk in faith and trust that, no matter what God asked of her, God would walk with her as she surrendered. As Mary modeled this faith and trust, Jesus also learned to walk in faith and trust.

There are many moments in the cancer journey when we have to surrender. We surrender our schedules and the illusion of control. We surrender our futures as we make the best decisions we can make with the information at hand.

We can't wait to see if there are future medical advances. We surrender our physical and emotional responses; we can't predict how our bodies will respond to treatment. We may know that "most people" respond well, but there is no guarantee that we are "most people." We surrender our "wanting a break" from medical issue after medical issue. We surrender with Mary.

Into every life, *suffering* comes. Mary suffered with Jesus as she watched the events leading up to the crucifixion. Mary suffered with Jesus as she held his dead body in her arms. Even though tears fell from Mary's eyes, she relied on her faith. She knew that eventually a tiny light would dispel the darkness. Our lives are filled with suffering that sometimes takes us by surprise. "You have a cancerous tumor." "You will lose your hair and be nauseated throughout the treatments." "Your energy level will be low, and you will have to learn to pace yourself." You feel the helplessness of others as they struggle to find words to comfort and console you. You feel your own helplessness as you push to respond as normally as possible to others. "Mrs. _____ just died and you had seen her the week before as you chatted during chemotherapy treatment." "I'm sorry; all we can offer is palliative care." We suffer like Mary.

Suffering challenges us to remain *faithful.* Mary walked with God throughout her entire journey. Walking in mystery was difficult. There were no answers to the many times she asked, "Why?" There were no answers to the many times she "pondered these things in her heart." Mary's soul remained faithful throughout all of the ups and downs in her life.

The cancer journey is filled with many questions that have no answers. As cancer patients we wonder: What if I had seen a doctor sooner? What if I had been more active? What will my friends and family do when I'm no longer around? How do I temper the urgency of life? How well am I walking the fine line of being independent while needing support? We remind each other—the whys and wherefores are not important but it is our ability to help each other remain faithful. Faithfulness is rooted in the prayers we receive from others as well as in the small distracted prayers we say for others. Faithfulness is found in the intimate chats we have with others as we explore the spiritual gifts that grow from this experience. Faithfulness is modeled by those who walked this path ahead of us; we remember the courage and determination of many of our friends and acquaintances. We walk in faithfulness with Mary.

The final jewel encompasses all of the other jewels. Mary was filled with *love* and Mary was led by Love. Every yes she uttered was based on a deep love for God, for her family, and for those with whom she came in contact. I imagine that as she made decisions, Mary based them on the question: "How does this deepen my love for others and for God?" She responded to everyone out of a deep compassion and love. As cancer patients, we too love much. When we first hear our diagnosis, many of us examine the love we have for family, friends, and God and base our decision to receive treatment on our love for those around us. We want more time to love longer.

As treatments begin and continue, they take a toll on everyone, but because of our deep love for each other, we are willing to overlook meltdowns and focus on the strong love that is present. Our love grows and deepens as we create new and often lasting relationships in our new communities formed in the infusion room or in cancer and/or ostomy support groups. I once read an epitaph that said, "She loved much." That phrase sums up Mary's life as well as most cancer survivors' lives. Everything Mary did was based on love; love can never be concealed. We love with Mary.

Prayer

Good and Gracious God, we praise and thank you for the many gifts you give us. Thank you especially for Mary, who teaches us how to walk with you. May we look to her in times of light and darkness, may she guide us during times of hope and despair, and may she give us faith and courage when we falter. May our love deepen as we journey toward eternity.

Journal Experience

Write a letter to Mary discussing each of the jewels and what each one means to you.

ALSO RECOMMENDED

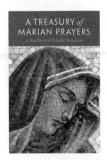

A Treasury of Marian Prayers
A Handbook of Popular Devotions
SR. JANET SCHAEFFLER, OP

We are gifted with many ways to pray with and to Mary. Arranged by topic and with fascinating background information, this beautiful book contains all the traditional Marian prayers and includes litanies, prayers that honor Mary's various titles, intercessory prayers, and many beloved prayers written by saints.

80 PAGES | $9.95 | 4" X 6" | 9781627852555

Hanging onto Hope
Reflections and Prayers for Finding "Good" in an Imperfect World
MELANNIE SVOBODA, SND

A flower growing through a crack in the sidewalk...two sparrows perched on a roof... Our world is yearning for signs of hope, and with images like these, Melannie Svoboda helps us open our hearts to hope, even in the darkest of times. Here, she explores the relationships between hope and faith, love, prayer, pain, and sorrow along with short prayers and questions for personal reflection or group sharing.

128 PAGES | $12.95 | 5½" X 8½" | 9781627853293

On Eagle's Wings
A Journey through Illness toward Healing
MICHAEL JONCAS

About ten years ago, Fr. Michael Joncas contracted Guillain-Barré syndrome, a debilitating physical condition that left this active teacher, musician, and liturgist weak and drained. The challenges and frustrations he experienced while on the road to recovery led to a time of deep spiritual insight. This book is the fruit of that discernment, offering five key spiritual insights to deepening one's relationship with God in times of darkness.

128 PAGES | $14.95 | 5½" X 8½" | 9781627852159

TO ORDER CALL 1-800-321-0411
OR VISIT WWW.23RDPUBLICATIONS.COM

TWENTY-THIRD PUBLICATIONS
A division of Bayard, Inc.